Toscani super DOC

8

Fabrizio Baroni

Granny's Recipes

*145 wholesome traditional Tuscan dishes
to relish all year round*

sarnus

www.sarnus.it

1st Italian edition: July 2012
1st Italian reprint: January 2013
1st English edition: September 2013

© 2013 EDIZIONI POLISTAMPA
   Via Livorno, 8/32 - 50142 Firenze
   Tel. 055 737871 (15 linee)
   info@polistampa.com - www.leonardolibri.com

ISBN 978-88-563-0149-6

Introduction

The title of this book is not a catchphrase, but simply the truth. The book was born out of the need to fix in time a part of an ancient culinary skill which has been transmitted from one generation of our family to the following. Hence, as dictated by my Grandmother, who is the last person of our family to hold such knowledge, I wrote the recipes, and took photos of a few prepared by herself. Granny, her name Giovannina Nencini, born in Mugello in 1921, is a housewife, with a lifelong passion for cooking. A passion transmitted by the elders of her family.

Nothing has been added to what could be retrieved from our personal knowledge: processes, combinations, methods strictly follow what has been handed down in our family up to Granny. If sometimes they do not coincide with the canonical recipes of traditional Tuscan cooking, we can assure you the result will always be excellent.

This book is a tribute to the ancient generations who cultivated and transmitted this wisdom, in particular to my Grandmother, who at the age of over eighty accepted my idea to compile this collection of recipes, and to prepare some for the photos. This is also a tribute to my Grandfather, who often helped her cook. The book is dedicated to the young generations who are losing this wisdom but want to recover it.

Since this collection of recipes is about the good things which compose our heritage, I don't limit myself to listing dishes that call for actual preparation or cooking, but include

– with the same importance and dignity – traditional combinations of foods for a snack, or a "tornagusto", as Collodi[1] called it. No cooking is required, but simply the bringing together of the right ingredients: for example broad beans and Pecorino cheese, bread and tomato, tuna fish and beans, with taste and wisdom, as the Italian families have always done and I hope they will continue to do.

The explanation of the recipes is minimal, the quantities of the ingredients are calculated for four people and are indicative only: everyone can adapt them according to personal taste. Where we mention olive oil, or simply oil, we always mean extra virgin of excellent quality.

Fabrizio Baroni

---

[1] Carlo Lorenzini (November 24, 1826 – October 26, 1890), better known by his pen name Carlo Collodi, was an Italian writer, famous for the world-renowned children novel, *The Adventures of Pinocchio*. "Tornagusto" means a food that tickles one's appetite.

PREFACE

Recently, a major American newspaper published an article claiming that good cooking in Italy is being threatened by the pace of life and work. According to the latest research, in Italy one third of the population is not interested in what they have on their plate. Despite this, pasta with tomato sauce, extra virgin olive oil, basil and the whole set of ingredients and knowledge that goes under the name of Mediterranean Cuisine has become part of the heritage of humanity, thanks to the decision, voted unanimously, of the UNESCO Committee! It was a choice that filled me too with profound emotion. But we can't but agree with the article in the American newspaper, which mentioned the risk of extinction of our everyday cookery, nutrition and care, handed down to daughters by their mothers (as well as grandmothers, aunts, nurses, cooks), following an all-female gastronomic heritage axis, generation after generation.

Bypassing gender boundaries and age-old traditions, we have to entrust men and women of the new generation, the so-called "orphans of the kitchen", with the task of recovering the principles of the culinary tradition. Still, the trouble with Italian cuisine is that it enjoys such an undisputed worldwide fame that admits no failures or steps back. Americans are surprised nowadays that the dishes cooked by Sophia Loren in movies are no longer our daily fare. Anyhow, the data of the first report on the eating habits of Italian people tell the story of a country dominated by the new "alimentary polytheism", as the researchers have baptised it. We have learned how to assemble goodies and habits, novelties and dietary concepts in a "perverse" mix which results in shopping trolleys and menus for authentic "taste schizophrenics". We buy biological superfresh and at the same time avalanches of canned food, pre-cooked and biodynamic food. We love the seasonal products of the farmer, but we eat exotic fruits and vegetables grown in greenhouses.

We demand a lot, but at the end of the day we are content with little. Nearly half of Italians consider themselves overweight and more than a third bitterly complain about not being able to eat more healthily. One in four would eat more fruit, honest to God, if only it cost less, while the consumption of the various stir-fry frozen foods, not exactly inexpensive, is in constant growth. To crown this alimentary hotch-patch, more than one third of the respondents are absolutely not interested in the quality of what they swallow daily. It's a red-alert percentage for the health of Italian people and consequently for the costs of the National Health Service, if it's true, as true it is, that risk factors related to obesity, cardiovascular problems, diabetes, hypertension, infarction, cancers and atherosclerosis correspond to approximately twenty-three billion Euro per year, of which more than sixty percent due to the increased spending on pharmaceuticals and hospital admissions. Correct, one may say, but the housewives of the past no longer exist, daughters of another time…

Well, that's why we, the Italians, in order to save the cost of eating out and to preserve our health, must restore a culture that is the envy of the world. All those willing and able, men and women alike, must return to the chopping-board. Fabrizio Baroni seems to welcome my invitation with

8

open arms, proposing a book that brings together the best culinary traditions inherited from his Grandmother and re-proposed in this fine little book. Here Tuscans and Italians can rediscover forgotten dishes and flavours of their child-hood, while our foreign friends can learn to enjoy tasty, colourful, simple, merry morsels that call for only a little good will and attention to enrich their table, to the benefit of health and the relief of the spirit.

Fabio Norcia
Nutritionist

PRAISE OF TUSCAN BREAD

This brief note aims to aid those who have no Tuscan bread available, to choose a kind of bread as similar as possible.

The typical Tuscan bread is a simple and rustic large, round loaf. It is characterized by the lack of salt, and the ingredients are wheat flour, water and brewer's yeast. It is preferably cooked in a wood-burning oven, and this way it can be kept for about a week.

In Tuscany cookery, bread has always played a central role, either fresh to accompany every kind of food like cheese, olive oil, beans, meats, jams, fruit, etc., or stale and used as an ingredient in a lot of traditional recipes, like the famous Ribollita. In fact, my family used to eat almost any food with bread. Tuscans were so true to bread, that all foods different from it were called "companatico", that means literally everything edible "that accompanies bread", reflecting its fundamental role.

GRANNY'S
RECIPES

STARTERS

BACCELLI COL PECORINO
Broad beans with Pecorino cheese

Unshelled fresh broad (fava) beans, 2 kg - Fresh Pecorino cheese, 400 g
Homemade Tuscan bread

Shell the broad beans and enjoy with some good fresh Pecorino cheese, and good fresh bread cut into slices. Doses are rather generous for a snack (200/250 g of broad beans can be obtained from 1 kg of unshelled fresh broad beans), but as we know, once you start you can't stop…

CROSTINI DI FEGATINI
Chicken liver croutons

1 stick of white bread, 350 g - Chicken livers, 300 g
1 fresh anchovy (or anchovy fillets in oil)
Half a red-skinned onion - Drained pickled capers, 20 g about
Meat stock, 2.5 dl - Tomato pulp - Olive oil - Salt

Chop the livers on the chopping board. Finely chop the onion and gently fry it in a pan with 3 tablespoons of olive oil, until transparent. Add the chopped livers and let them brown. Moisten with *meat stock* or *vegetable stock* (see recipes), add a teaspoon of tomato pulp and the anchovy previously filleted and chopped: salt with care.

Stir until the anchovy is melted. After about 20 minutes from the start of cooking, over a gentle heat, the mixture should be similar to a homogeneous amalgam: just before the end of cooking, add the chopped capers. Cut the bread into thin slices, slightly toast and moisten them in the stock on one side only, barely touching it, otherwise they will tend to disintegrate.

Some people moisten the browning livers with a little wine, then add a little hot stock while cooking, if they tend to get dry. These traditional croutons can become part of a lunch for special occasions, for example Christmas and New Year, consisting primarily of our croutons, followed by Tortellini in stock, boiled meat, stuffed chicken neck, green sauce, boiled vegetables, and a cake freely chosen from the Tuscan Tradition, all accompanied of course by some good Tuscan bread.

FETTE COL CAVOLO NERO
Bread slices with kale

4 slices of homemade Tuscan bread
2 bunches of Tuscan dark green cabbage, or kale - 1 garlic clove
Excellent olive oil, freshly pressed - Salt and pepper

Wash the cabbage leaves (preferably that have "felt" the cold winter nights) and boil them in boiling salted water for about 20 minutes. It is better to start with already warm water, in order to minimize the time of immersion of the cabbage, so that it preserves its substances as much as possible; the same applies to any other vegetable.

Toast the slices of bread, preferably a little stale, rub with a peeled clove of garlic and moisten with the stock of the cabbage, still hot.

Lay one or more squeezed cabbage leaves on each slice and season with plenty of oil, salt and pepper. They are meant to be served hot, and, in spite of the simplicity of the recipe, the taste is amazing!

FETTUNTA
Toasted bread with oil

4 slices of fresh homemade bread - 1 garlic clove
Excellent olive oil, freshly pressed - Salt and pepper

Toast the slices of bread on both sides, until they are wonderfully crunchy and rub with a peeled clove of garlic on both sides. Season them with olive oil, salt and pepper. The toast should be eaten when the bread is still warm. Another favourite is *bread and oil*, which is nothing more than a slice of fresh bread sprinkled with salt and dribbled with oil, ideal for snacks.

FIORI DI ZUCCA FRITTI
Fried courgette flowers

16 courgette flowers - 2 eggs - Wheat flour, 150 g
Oil for deep-frying - Salt

Wash the courgette flowers, remove the pistil and dry with a cloth. Dredge them with flour, dip in beaten egg and, finally, deep-fry a few at a time until they are golden and crisp in hot oil: take them out as they are ready with a skimmer, depositing them on an absorbent paper towel, salting them to taste.

A variation of this recipe is to place a salted anchovy fillet of appropriate dimensions inside each flower.

PANE, BURRO E ACCIUGHE
Bread, butter and anchovy

4 slices of fresh homemade bread - 8 salted anchovies - Butter

Remove the salt from the anchovies without washing and fillet them. Spread the butter on the slices of bread and lay the fillets on them. Despite its simplicity, the combination of the taste of butter and anchovies makes this starter a delicacy for connoisseurs! With butter and anchovies you can also prepare some croutons to serve with *chicken liver croutons* (see recipe).

PANE FRITTO
Fried bread

4 slices of fresh or slightly stale bread - 2 eggs - Flour, 200 g
Oil for deep-frying - Salt

Slice the bread, dip slices first in the beaten eggs and then dredge with flour, and finally deep-fry them. Drain and put to dry on an absorbent paper towel: salt to taste. The fried bread can be a great accompaniment to other fried meat-based dishes, for example *fried chops* or *fried chicken* (see recipes).

For a crisper result, some prefer not to flour the slices of bread.

Fried, even a slipper is good!

~~~~~

PANE, OLIO E POMODORO
Bread, oil and tomato

4 slices of fresh homemade bread - 2 ripe tomatoes
Olive oil - Salt and pepper

Wash the tomatoes, cut them in half and rub on the bread slices. If you don't like tomato seeds, remove them before rubbing. Season with plenty of oil, salt and pepper. To make the slices more substantial, you can also cut thin slices of tomato and lay them on top of the bread. This is definitely a delicious summer snack.

A bit of bread, a good "companatico" [2] and... enjoy! When a steaming meat sauce is ready (see recipe), for example, who can resist the temptation to spread a little over a slice of fresh bread?

---

[2] "Companatico" means anything that accompanies bread during the meal. This definition emphasizes the great importance of bread in Tuscany.

PINZIMONIO
Oil dip

4 artichokes - 2 fennel bulbs - 2 celery stalks
4 spring onions - Lemon juice - Olive oil
Salt and pepper

Remove chewy outer leaves of the artichokes, one by one, and also the thorns. Cut down the harder stalks of the fennels and slice the "heart" lengthwise. Eliminate the "beards" of the onions and remove both ends of the celery stalks: wash all parts freshly prepared and dry them well. Prepare plenty of oil in a bowl with lemon juice, salt and pepper, dip in the vegetables and bite to enjoy!

~～~

PROSCIUTTO E POPONE
Ham and melon

1 cantaloupe melon - Tuscan raw ham, 250 g
Tuscan homemade bread

Cold summer dish, at the time of ripe melons. Cut the melon in two lengthwise, remove the seeds inside, cut the two halves into wedges and serve with slices of ham cut by hand, with plenty of good fresh bread.

SALAME E FICHI
Salami and figs

Tuscan salami, 250 g - A dozen fresh ripe figs
Tuscan homemade bread

Another cold summer dish, in the season of figs. Slice the salami by hand and cut the figs lenghwise into four cloves: once again, serve with good Tuscan bread, sliced.

SALVIA FRITTA
Fried sage

24 large leaves of sage - 12 anchovy fillets in salt
2 eggs - Wheat flour, 200 g - Oil for deep-frying - Salt

Make a kind of sandwich by laying a fillet between two large leaves of sage. Repeat until all ingredients are used: dredge the "sandwiches" with flour, then in the beaten egg and deep-fry in plenty of hot oil. Take them out when they are golden, place them to dry on absorbent paper towel and salt to taste. To complete the dish, you can also fry some leaves of sage dredging them in flour and egg, but without the anchovy. Some nice large basil leaves can also be fried in the same way.

TRIPPA PREZZEMOLATA
Parsley tripe

Tripe, 500 g - 1 garlic clove
A bunch of parsley - Olive oil - Salt and pepper

Wash the tripe, drain and cut into thin strips: season with salt and pepper, sprinkle with finely chopped garlic and parsley, pour in a little olive oil and stir. From cold tripe, without further cooking, a richer dish can be made, *tripe salad*, adding pitted olives, chopped onions, peppers cut into small pieces, and other ingredients depending on your taste.

And if you want to taste the tripe as a rich dish, the solution is Florentine tripe *(see recipe). Tripe is a typical Tuscan street-food. It's made from edible offal from the stomachs of ruminants, previously boiled and blanched. In Florence the most popular cuts of tripe, obtained from the omasum, are called "cuffia" (reticulum) and "croce" (rumen). Also very popular is "lampredotto", i.e. the abomasum of cattle.*

SAUCES AND STOCKS

ACCIUGATA
Anchovy sauce

5 salted anchovies - Drained pickled capers, 30 g - 1 garlic clove
Parsley - Olive oil - Pepper

Remove the salt from the anchovies and fillet them. Finely chop
parsley, capers and garlic. Chop the anchovy fillets and set them gently to fry in the oil, stirring continuously until they are melted. Add
the chopped vegetables, keep on the heat for a few minutes more and
the sauce is ready: finish with a pinch of pepper (salt not needed).

*The anchovy sauce is delicious for dressing hard-boiled eggs, pasta,
rice, boiled meat, fried chops. In case of pasta, cook "al dente"[3] 350 g of
spaghetti (you don't need to salt the water, because the salt of the anchovies will be sufficient), drain and season with plenty of anchovy
sauce.*

TUSCAN BESCIAMELLA
Bechamel Tuscan style

Milk, half a litre - Wheat flour, 40 g - Butter, 35 g - Salt, pepper

These quantities are calculated for about half a litre of
bechamel. Melt the butter gently in a saucepan, add the flour

---

[3] "Al dente" means that you must stop boiling the pasta a little before it is
completely cooked.

21

and stir, taking care to avoid lumps. When the mixture begins to turn brown, add the milk gradually at room temperature and let it thicken: keep stirring, and don't forget to season with salt and pepper. After 20 minutes your bechamel is ready.

Everyone believes that bechamel is a French recipe, actually – as local tradition holds – it seems to have been conceived in Florence, under the name of "salsa colla" (literally, glue sauce), and then exported to France by Caterina de' Medici[4].

BRODO DI CARNE
Meat stock

Beef (muscle, brisket or chin, chuck, spongy bone, etc.), 500 g
Half a hen (better if old, in agreement with the old Italian proverb!)
1 carrot - 1 red onion - 1 celery stalk - 4 small ripe tomatoes
Parsley - Salt

Put herbs and meat in a pot filled with cold water, turn on the heat and boil very slowly for at least 2 hours. When you remove the meat and the herbs, let the stock cool for a while and

---

[4] Caterina de' Medici, (13 April 1519-5 January 1589), daughter of Lorenzo II de' Medici and of Madeleine de La Tour d'Auvergne, was a Franco/Italian noblewoman who was Queen consort of France from 1547 until 1559, as the wife of King Henry II of Valois. Her great-grandfather Lorenzo de' Medici was an Italian statesman and de facto ruler of the Florentine Republic during the Italian Renaissance (from wikipedia).

remove the layer of fat on the surface with a skimmer. Finally, strain the stock through a sieve to remove the remains of the herbs. As for the hen, we recommend not removing the skin and the head, because they give flavour to the stock, and when boiled are very good to eat.

This beef stock can be used for making soups and cooking Tortellini, preparing chicken liver croutons *(see recipe) and can also be enjoyed hot in a cup as a nutritious drink. To make the stock into soup special pasta shapes are needed (which in Italy have curious names, such as "capelli d'angelo", angel's hair, or "grandinina", small hail grains, and similar) in a ratio of approximately 30 g per person for dry pasta and 50 g for egg. The boiled meat is obviously not thrown away, but can be enjoyed garnished with* green sauce *or following the recipes of "rifatto" or* re-cooked boiled beef *and* meatballs *(see recipes). The same applies to the boiled hen, which can be seasoned with oil or* green sauce.

<h2 style="text-align:center">The old hen makes good broth!</h2>

BRODO VEGETALE
Vegetable stock

1 carrot - 1 red onion - 1 celery stalk - 1 garlic clove
4 ripe cherry tomatoes - Parsley - Salt

Put all vegetables chopped into small pieces into cold water. Boil for about an hour with a pinch of salt and the stock is ready.

It is remarkable that from vegetables alone, you can get an intensity of flavour that, at least in our opinion, is by no means inferior to what you get using meat also. To enhance the result, you can remove the boiled vegetables from the stock and squeeze them with a fork on the bottom of a colander. Vegetable stock can be used to make soups and in the preparation of dishes that require the addition of liquids, such as rice first courses: it can also be savoured hot on its own as an invigorating drink.

CONSERVA DI POMODORO
Tomato preserve

Ripe Florentine ribbed tomatoes[5], about 2 kg

Among the many varieties of tomatoes, if you have it available, we suggest you use the juicy Florentine ribbed tomato. Blanch tomatoes in boiling water, drain and press them through the tomato crusher, which also separates the pulp from the peel. Put the pulp in a saucepan and bring to the boil for a short time. Place a clean cloth over a colander of appropriate size and pour the hot pulp in, letting it strain through the fabric for about a quarter of an hour. Put the filtered pulp in hermetic-seal glass jars, then set them to boil, totally covered with water, for about 20 minutes. This tomato preserve is basically a homemade tomato concentrate, that can be very useful in many recipes. But take care not to exaggerate: a small amount is quite enough to flavour a dish!

---

[5] Florentine ribbed tomato is a variety characterized by the presence of ribs, as if it were divided into cloves. If not available, you can of course use other varieties, such as Aker's West Viginia, Brandywine, Church or similar.

Antique preparation for solid preserve: *press blanched tomatoes in the tomato crusher. Stretch out a cloth between two chairs, after having washed it in vinegar, and pour over the paste. Wait for about 2 days, until it is well drained, and then put to dry in the oven at a low temperature, until all moisture is gone. Store in tightly sealed glass jars.*

SALSA DI POMODORO
Tomato sauce

Ripe Florentine ribbed tomatoes, 1 kg - 1 carrot - 1 red onion - 1 celery stalk - 2 garlic cloves - A sprig of basil - 1 chili pepper - Olive oil - Salt

As in previous recipe, we recommend using Florentine ribbed tomatoes, if you can find them. Cut the tomatoes in halves, deseed them, chop into small pieces and place in a pan. Add chopped vegetables, i.e. carrot, onion, celery without leaves, garlic and basil, add chopped chili pepper without seeds, pour in a little olive oil, salt and put to boil over a low heat for about an hour.

Storage: put your tomato sauce into glass jars and pour a little oil over the surface, so that it forms a sort of natural cap. Close the jars tight and store: after you re-open one, you should keep it in the fridge. Use the sauce to flavour a good dish of pasta (350 g for four people), adding some coarsely chopped basil leaves: sprinkle with grated Parmesan cheese.

SALSA VERDE
Green sauce
(Granny's style)

Drained pickled capers, 40 g
A bunch of parsley, 50 g
A sprig of basil - Garlic (see below)
Olive oil - Salt and pepper

Chop the herbs very finely, adding only a quarter of a garlic clove, otherwise it will tend to dominate in the flavour of the sauce. Add plenty of good oil, stirring it in well and season with salt and pepper.

This sauce is ideal as a garnish for braised or boiled meat (preferably cold), boiled salt cod (see recipes), as well as pasta, or it can be spread on slices of fresh bread. The traditional recipe for green sauce, which is made without the basil, uses a little hard-boiled egg, anchovy fillets and breadcrumbs, giving more room to the garlic (one clove at least): no objections, but try our version and savour the lightness and the tantalizing smell...

SUGO DI CARNE
Meat sauce

Minced beef, 400 g - Tomato pulp, 200 g - 2 garlic cloves
1 carrot - 1 red onion - 2 celery stalks - Parsley - Rosemary
Red wine - Olive oil - Salt and pepper

The beef has should be lean and finely minced. Chop garlic, onion, celery, carrot and rosemary and gently brown them in a little oil in a saucepan. As soon as they are brown, add the minced beef and stir throughly. Once the meat starts to turn brown, pour on half a glass of wine and raise the heat. Add the tomato pulp and enough water: season with salt and pepper and let the meat sauce boil slowly for at least half an hour.

Meat sauce can be used to garnish "penne strascicate" and polenta (cornmeal), for baked pasta, for rabbit or chicken stew (see recipes), but also to dip a slice of good bread into and whatever other uses your imagination can suggest.

FIRST COURSES

GNOCCHI DI FARINA GIALLA
Cornmeal dumplings

Cornmeal flour, 300 g - Meat sauce (see recipe)
Grated Parmesan cheese - Salt

Put lightly salted water to boil in a pot (the proportion is a litre of water for every 250 g of flour). Add cornmeal to the boiling water, stirring constantly to prevent lumps forming. Keep on cooking for half an hour, always stirring, to prevent it sticking and burning on the bottom of the pot.

When cooked, make the "dumplings" by taking spoonfuls of the cornmeal with a wet tablespoon, arrange them on plates alternating with layers of meat sauce and sprinkle over the grated cheese. As an alternative to meat sauce, you can garnish with *tomato sauce* (see recipe) and grated Parmesan cheese.

GNOCCHI DI PATATE (TOPINI)
Potato dumplings

Floury potatoes, 1 kg
Wheat flour, 250 g
(in addition to that necessary for dusting the pastry board)
1 egg - Salt

Potato dumplings are also known to Tuscans as "topini", i.e. little mice. Boil potatoes and peel them: transfer them to a large bowl and mash gradually adding the flour and beaten egg, until you obtain a firm but not pasty dough, that must not stick to your fingers. Wet your hands and take small pieces of the dough, roll them on a clean floured tea towel into "sticks" of about 1 cm in diameter, then chop into pieces to make the dumplings. If you want to give them the typical ribbed appearance, roll each well-floured dumpling over the hollow back of a cheese grater.

Cooking: put the dumplings all together in salted boiling water, wait until they come to the surface and the water returns to the boil. At this point, you are over with the cooking: take them out with the skimmer draining then as you go and garnish to taste.

Be careful, because the cooking time is very short. You can serve them simply with butter or any sauce, for example tomato sauce *or* meat sauce *(see recipes) and a good sprinkling of Parmesan cheese.*

Flour, with just a little water added, was the basic ingredient of "farinata", a homemade baby gruel that, up to a few decades ago, was the typical nourishment of weaned children, perhaps no worse than many commercial baby foods...

MINESTRA DI FAGIOLI
Bean soup

Fresh Cannellini beans, 500 g - Ribbed pasta tubes, 200 g
1 garlic clove - Rosemary - Sage - Olive oil - Salt

Put the beans to boil in cold water with a few leaves of sage and salt for about 2 hours; make sure to cover the pot and keep the heat as low as possible: when they are cooked, pass them through a food mill and put the paste back into the pot.

Fry the whole clove of garlic and the chopped rosemary in a little oil. Remove the garlic, add the scented oil to the mashed beans, add water as needed, so that the soup is neither too liquid nor too thick, and cook the pasta in it.

The same procedure applies to chickpea soup: *ingredients and quantities are the same, replacing the fresh beans with 300 g of dried chickpeas previously soaked for at least 8 hours. Boil the chickpeas, mash them, add the scented oil, and enough water to cook the pasta.*

Some people prefer not to mash all the legumes, but leave some whole, to make the dish more attractive. If you like, a nice trickle of good olive oil on each steaming bowl of soup is a nice finish.

MINESTRA DI PORRI
Leek soup

Leeks, 1 kg - Vegetable stock (see recipe), 1.5 l - Tomato pulp
Olive oil - Salt and pepper

Trim the leeks, cut them into thin slices and cook in the vegetable stock with a little tomato pulp (very little!) and oil for about half an hour. Add the salt, and the soup is ready.

When you serve this soup, you can add some grated Parmesan cheese and some toasted slices of stale homemade bread, rubbed with a peeled clove of garlic, which makes this simple dish more filling and pleasant.

MINESTRA DI PANE
Bread soup

Stale homemade Tuscan bread, 250 g - Cannellini beans, 500 g
2 potatoes - 2 courgettes - Half a savoy cabbage - 1 leek - 2 carrots
1 red onion - 1 celery stalk - A bunch of Tuscan "black" cabbage or kale
1 garlic clove - Tomato pulp, 50 g - Olive oil - Salt

Pass the boiled beans through a food mill, except for a few: pour the paste into the cooking water of the beans. Chop onion, garlic, leek, one carrot, celery, and sauté; when slightly browned, add the second carrot chopped into chunks. Add the bean paste with their water, the whole beans and the tomato pulp. Bring gently to the boil: then add "black" cabbage or kale, savoy cabbage, potatoes and courgettes chopped into small pieces, and leave to simmer for about 2 hours, adding the salt.

Finally, cut the bread into thin slices, add it to the cooking soup and stir until ready.

Cook this soup in the evening for the next day's lunch, or in the morning for supper. Warm it up gently for 10 minutes before serving. The taste leaves people astonished.

These quantities are generous, but, as everyone knows, it is enough to re-boil left-over bread soup to transform it into the famous Ribollita.

MINESTRONE
Vegetable soup

2 potatoes - 3 courgettes - Half a savoy cabbage
Shelled green peas, 150 g
A small bunch of Tuscan "black" cabbage or kale
A bunch of chard - 1 leek - 1 carrot - 1 red onion
2 celery stalks - Salt and pepper

Wash the vegetables, cut into small pieces and put to boil slowly in salted water for about an hour, starting from cold. Season with salt and pepper and stir often with a wooden spoon.

This soup can be tasted as it is, even lukewarm or cold, or you can add boiled short soup pasta or rice, or toasted slices of bread. If you pass it through a food mill you get a good vegetable puree *to make savoury soups, by cooking pasta in it.*

PANZANELLA
Bread salad

Stale homemade Tuscan bread, 500 g - 1 red onion
1 cucumber - 3 salted anchovies (or fillets in oil)
Drained pickled capers, 30 g - Basil - Vinegar
Olive oil - Salt and pepper

Panzanella is a typical summer dish. Soak the bread (preferably very stale) in cold water for about half an hour, squeeze it well, crumble and place in a bowl. Take care to squeeze all water out of the bread, otherwise it remains wet and, even worse, leaves a layer of water in the bottom of the bowl. This is the main possible failure of panzanella. Roughly chop onion, cucumber and filleted anchovies and add to the soaked bread. Add capers, chopped basil and season with vinegar, salt, pepper and a drizzle of oil. If you have time, put it in the fridge and serve cold.

Traditional panzanella is made using only bread, onion, ripe tomato (the salad not the sauce variety) and basil, but it is the habit

34

of every family "to customize" it and to enrich to taste, for example with lettuce, tuna fish in oil, pitted olives, or Pecorino cheese, radishes and celery hearts: chacun sa façon...

PAPPA AL POMODORO
Tomato and bread soup

Stale homemade Tuscan bread, 300 g
Ripe Florentine ribbed tomatoes, 300 g
Vegetable stock, 1 l - 3 garlic cloves
Basil - Olive oil - Salt and pepper

As for tomatoes, if available, you should use as usual Florentine ribbed tomatoes, or reliable substitutes: wash them, cut in half, deseed, chop into small pieces and put to boil in stock with garlic, basil and a little salt, for about half an hour at a medium heat.

Meanwhile, cut the bread into small pieces, or thin slices, trying to crumble the crust. Add the bread to the cooking tomato and continue to boil for another 10 minutes: keep stirring, until the bread turns into a mush.

Let it rest for about 20 minutes, to "revive" the bread: at the time of serving, garnish with olive oil of excellent quality.

Opinions about the correct proportions of tomato to bread vary greatly. Some people like the soup very red, with a lot of tomato,

35

some opt for an almost imperceptible quantity. Decide according to your taste.

Some people cook the tomato in water, but with vegetable stock the result is much richer.

PASTA AL FORNO
DI CASA NOSTRA
Baked lasagne
Granny style

Egg lasagne, 350 g
Meat sauce (see recipe), 250 g
Bechamel (see recipe), 8 dl
Mozzarella, 250 g
Butter - Salt

Blanch the lasagne in lightly salted boiling water, take them out with a fish slice, drain and lay without overlapping on a clean cloth to dry.

Take a rectangular roasting pan, butter it and spread on the bottom a thin layer of meat sauce followed by a layer of pasta and a layer of bechamel, adding a few slices of mozzarella, then another layer of sauce and so on, until all ingredients are used up.

Put the pan in the oven at 160 °C for three quarters of an hour. Cut the baked pasta into rectangles and serve.

PASTE AL SUGO DI CIPOLLE
Pasta with onion sauce

Short pasta, 350 g - 2 onions
Olive oil - Salt

Peel the onions, removing roots and outer skin. Cut them into very thin slices and place them to sweat in oil in a saucepan with lid, making sure they don't turn brown. Cook slowly for about half an hour, adding salt and a little water or vegetable stock if necessary, until they become a uniform paste. At this point they are ready for dressing the pasta, that in the meantime you have cooked and drained. You can choose whether to add some Parmesan cheese or not, according to taste.

PASTE AL SUGO DI MELANZANA
Pasta with aubergine sauce

Long pasta, 350 g - 1 aubergine
1 garlic clove - Tomato pulp, as required
1 chili pepper - Parsley - Basil
Grated Parmesan cheese
Olive oil - Coarse and fine salt

Peel the aubergine, cut into thin slices and place in a deep tray, covered with coarse salt, for a few hours: then wash the salt off, dry slices thoroughly and brown them on both sides in a pan with 4 tablespoons of olive oil, over a lively heat.

Chop garlic, parsley, basil and pepper, place in a saucepan with a film of oil: add a tablespoon of tomato pulp and the browned aubergine slices, adding salt. Cook over medium heat for a quarter of an hour, stirring: at this point the aubergines have almost disintegrated, forming a quite smooth paste. Garnish the pasta with this sauce: it's great with a sprinkle of grated cheese.

PENNE STRASCICATE
Pasta "dragged" in meat sauce

"Penne" (ribbed short pasta), 350 g
Meat sauce (see recipe), 250 g
Grated Parmesan cheese
Salt

Cook the "penne" in plenty of lightly salted water and drain them well "al dente" (a little before you would normally). Tip them into a saucepan where you have heated plenty of good home-made meat sauce. Stir them vigorously into the sauce over a high heat, coating them thoroughly, sprinkle generously with grated cheese, stir again, turn off the heat and serve.

Why "dragged" pasta? Because the pasta is literally "dragged" through the meat sauce to be dressed!

38

POLENTA
Cornmeal

Cornmeal, 300 g
Salt

As described in the recipe for Cornmeal Dumplings, put lightly salted water to boil in a large saucepan (the proportion is a litre of water for 250 g of flour). Add the cornmeal to the boiling water, and stir constantly to prevent the forming of lumps.

Keep cooking this way for about 40 minutes, stirring constantly, to prevent the meal sticking to the bottom of the pot and getting burned.

When cooked, "polenta" should have become stiff. Tip it onto a cloth, cover and let it cool before serving.

To really enjoy polenta, cut it into slices using a wire held taut between your hands and eat it just as it is, hot or cold.

But there are many ways to garnish it and make it more appetizing. Shall we mention a few? Serve polenta *with* meat sauce *and a good sprinkling of Parmesan cheese, or with* tomato sauce *(see recipes), again sprinkled with cheese, or simply with a sprinkling of Parmesan cheese (or mature Pecorino cheese), or with some nice boiled "black" Tuscan cabbage or kale leaves and a drizzle of good olive oil.*

RISO AI CARCIOFI
Rice with artichokes

Short-grain (Arborio) rice, 300 g
4 small violet artichokes, 300 g
1 garlic clove - Parsley - Olive oil - Salt and pepper

Remove the tough outer leaves from the artichokes, trim the tops and finely chop the artichokes, garlic and parsley, also using the tender part of the stems. Gently fry in a little oil for a few minutes, add a bit of hot water (or vegetable stock) and cook for a quarter of an hour. Then add the rice and sufficient hot water (or vegetable stock, for an even tastier result) to cook it, season with salt and pepper. Just before serving make sure that the dish is neither too liquid nor too dry.

And here we are in the realm of rice, nutritious and easy to digest, very good boiled in stock, in "risotto" recipes or served with a range of sauces: with plenty of olive oil, grated Parmesan cheese and pepper, or with an excellent tomato sauce *(see recipe) and chopped basil leaves, with* porcino mushrooms *(see recipe), or with an aromatic* anchovy sauce *(see recipe). Remember that, instead of water, rice can be cooked in* vegetable stock *(see recipe) to make the dish even tastier.*

RISO AI PORRI
Rice with leeks

Short-grain (Arborio) rice, 300 g - 4 leeks
1 garlic clove - Parsley - Olive oil - Salt and pepper

Clean leeks and chop finely with garlic and parsley, gently sauté the chopped vegetables for a few minutes in a little oil, add a little hot water (or vegetable stock) and cook for a quarter of an hour. Then add the rice, sufficient hot water (or vegetable stock, for an even tastier result) to cook it, adding salt and pepper. In this case too, just before serving, make sure that the dish is neiter too liquid nor too dry.

SPAGHETTI AGLIO, OLIO E PEPERONCINO
Garlic, oil and chili pepper spaghetti

Spaghetti, 250 g - 1 garlic clove - 4 red chili peppers
Olive oil - Salt

Bring to the boil a pot with enough salted water to cook the spaghetti. Sauté the finely chopped garlic and chili pepper (with seeds removed) in oil poured generously into a pan of appropriate size, but don't overdo it. Drain the spaghetti "al dente" and transfer them to the pan, allow the flavours to merge over a high heat, stirring well.

Those who do not like garlic can put it whole to fry in oil and remove it prior to garnishing the pasta. The spaghetti should not be broken, but simply put in the boiling pot resting on the edges: as they soften, they slide down into the boiling water by themselves, with the help of the spoon if necessary.

SPAGHETTI AL SUGO DI TONNO
Tuna fish spaghetti

Spaghetti, 350 g - Tuna fish in oil, 200 g
1 garlic clove - Parsley
Tomato preserve (see recipe) - Olive oil - Salt and pepper

Bring to the boil a pot with enough salted water to cook the spaghetti. Drain the tuna fish, chop it with garlic and parsley and warm it up in a pan with a little oil. Add a tablespoon of *tomato preserve* (or a teaspoon of tomato paste), a little hot water and allow the flavours to merge for 10 minutes, adding salt and pepper. Drain the spaghetti "al dente" and garnish with the sauce.

⌒⌒⌒

SPAGHETTI ALLE VONGOLE
Spaghetti with clams

Spaghetti, 350 g - Shelled clams, 200 g
Tomato pulp (see below)
1 garlic clove - 1 chili pepper
Parsley - Olive oil
Salt

Bring to the boil in good time a pot with enough salted water to cook the spaghetti. Chop garlic, parsley and chili (seeds removed): gently sauté this mixture in a pan with a little oil, add the clams and let the flavours merge for one minute over high heat. Add a tablespoon of tomato pulp and let sauce thicken over low heat for 10 minutes.

Drain the spaghetti "al dente", transfer them to the pan and let them flavour briefly over a high heat, stirring well.

TORTELLI DI PATATE
Potato "Tortelli" (large ravioli)

Wheat flour, 400 g (in addition to that required for preparation)
4 medium floury potatoes
1 egg - A sprig of parsley
Meat sauce (for the dressing, see recipe)
Grated Parmesan cheese - Salt and pepper

Prepare the dough on the floured pastry board by mixing flour and egg with a pinch of salt, and sufficient water to produce a smooth and elastic dough. Shape into a ball, and leave to rest in a cool place wrapped in a clean cloth.

Meanwhile, you need to boil the potatoes: peel them still hot, mash and mix with 4 tablespoons of grated Parmesan cheese, chopped parsley, salt and pepper. If the filling is left over, don't worry: it is good to eat just as it is!

Roll out the dough and cut it into not too thin strips, about double the width of the tortelli, i.e. 10 cm and sprinkle with flour. Pick up a little ball of filling and lay it down on one side of the strip: place other balls at regular distances on the strips of dough until you run out of filling. Fold the other edge of the strip over and press the edges with a fork to seal them. Cut out the tortelli using a pastrywheel. As you go along, place the finished tortelli side by side on a clean slightly floured cloth. Cook the tortelli in lightly salted boiling water for 5 minutes, removing them with the skimmer as they come to the surface. Season to taste and enjoy.

The ideal condiment is meat sauce *(see recipe), but they are also excellent served with butter and sage. If you choose meat sauce, place the tortelli in a bowl in alternate layers with the sauce and a sprinkling of grated cheese.*

ZUPPA DI CIPOLLE
Onion soup

6 red onions
4 slices of homemade bread
Olive oil - Grated Parmesan cheese
Salt and pepper

Gently fry thinly-sliced onions in a little oil in a pan. Let them sweat over a low heat, stirring. Add some hot water and carry on cooking for at least an hour. Season with salt and pepper.

Toast the slices of bread, place them in the bowls and pour over the hot soup. If you wish, sprinkle with grated cheese.

To give more flavour to the dish, you can add some vegetable stock instead of water. Red onions can be substituted with white ones, or if you like, with leeks.

ZUPPA LOMBARDA
"Lombard" bean soup

Boiled white beans, 500 g
4 slices of stale homemade bread
Olive oil
Salt and pepper

First, you need to boil the beans with a sprig of sage (for cooking, see the recipe for "Fagioli all'olio"). Toast the slices of bread, put them in the bowls and pour over the hot cooking stock of the beans with a few of beans themselves and a sage leaf. Pour over plenty of oil, season with salt and pepper.

FISH AND MOLLUSKS

ACCIUGHE FRITTE
Fried anchovies

2 dozens fresh anchovies - Wheat flour, 150 g
1 lemon - Oil for deep-frying - Salt

Clean the anchovies (just open the belly with your thumb nail to extract the innards), wash and put to dry on a cloth. Flour them, shaking to remove the excess, and deep-fry in plenty of hot oil: remove with the skimmer as soon they are golden and crisp, and place them on absorbent paper towel. Salt and, if you like, sprinkle with squeezed lemon. They are best warm, but remain good even cold.

We recommend not filleting anchovies, and not even removing the heads: it's all tasty. Alternatively to anchovies, you can deep-fry other varieties of blue and white fish of small size, for example, silversides, sardines and whitebait. Of course, the larger the size, the longer the frying time.

He who sleeps doesn't catch fish

ARINGHE ALLA BRACE
Grilled herrings

Smoked or fresh herrings (1 kg, if fresh; 700 g, if smoked fillets) - 1 carrot
A piece of lemon peel - Parsley - Drained pickled capers, 30 g - Olive oil - Salt

Roast the herrings over the embers. Separately chop carrot, parsley, lemon peel and capers to be spread on the herrings and dress them with a little olive oil. Salt only if they are fresh.

ARINGHE MARINATE SOTT'OLIO
Marinated herrings in oil

4 smoked herring fillets, 600 g - 1 garlic clove - 1 celery stalk
1 carrot - Half an onion - Parsley - Milk, 2.5 dl - Olive oil

Dip herring fillets in milk and let them soak for a few hours. Roughly chop garlic, celery, carrot, onion and parsley. Drain the fillets and place in a deep bowl: sprinkle with the chopped herbs and cover with oil.

ARSELLE
Tellin or clam stew

Tellins or clams, 1.8 kg - Tomato pulp, 200 g - 1 onion - 1 celery stalk
2 garlic cloves - Rosemary - Parsley - Red chili pepper
Olive oil - Salt

Wash the shellfish keeping them in water for about half a day, so that they can expel the sand. Finely chop onion, garlic, rosemary, parsley, red chili pepper and celery: gently sauté in a little oil and add tomato pulp, letting the flavours blend. Add the shellfish and cook over a low heat for about a quarter of an hour, adding salt and a little water if necessary. You can savour the shellfish by sucking the mollusk directly from the shell as from a spoon, or shelled, with their cooking juices, or spread on slices of toasted bread.

❧

BACCALÀ ALLA LIVORNESE
Salt cod Leghorn style

Soaked salt cod, 800 g
Tomato pulp, 350 g
1 garlic clove - Parsley - Wheat flour, 180 g
Olive oil - Pepper

Cut the cod into large pieces, dredge with flour and, in a pan with a film of oil, fry it for a few minutes on either side until golden. Remove with the skimmer and place them to dry on absorbent paper towel. Meanwhile, peel the garlic and gently sweat in a pan with 3 tablespoons of olive oil. Add tomato and then let sauce thicken briefly with a pinch of pepper: salt only if necessary. After 5 minutes, add the cod and let the flavours blend slowly for a quarter of an hour. Add chopped parsley towards the end of cooking and serve.

We strongly recommend not removing the skin of the cod, as we do believe it's the most delicious part of all.

Cod, liver and eggs, the longer you cook, the tougher they are.

BACCALÀ FRITTO
Fried salt cod

Soaked salt cod, 800 g - Wheat flour - 1 lemon - Oil for deep-frying

Cut cod into pieces, flour them and deep-fry in plenty of hot oil until nicely golden, so that it is crunchy outside and juicy inside. Remove with the skimmer, lay it down to dry on absorbent paper towel. At the end, sprinkle with the juice of a squeezed lemon, if you like, according to your taste.

As an alternative to simple flouring, you can prepare a batter with flour, water and a little oil and dip the pieces of cod into it.

BACCALÀ "IN INZIMINO" COL PORRO
Salt cod stew with chard and leek

Soaked salt cod, 500 g
Chard leaves, 600 g - 1 leek
Tomato preserve (see recipe) - Olive oil - Pepper

Blanch chard leaves in lightly salted boiling water, drain, squeeze and chop. Cut the cod into pieces and sauté it for 5 minutes, with the leek chopped into strips, in a pan with a little oil, over a low flame. Add the chard with a teaspoon of tomato preserve and cook slowly for another 5-10 minutes, adding pepper to taste.

Leek instead of the traditional fried garlic, in addition to replacing tomato pulp with a little tomato preserve, are Granny's variations on the canonical recipe: a good idea, indeed, you will taste what a treat!

BACCALÀ LESSO
Boiled salt cod

Soaked salt cod, 800 g - 1 lemon - Olive oil - Pepper

Place the cod in a pan of cold water and bring to the boil over a low heat, continuing for about 10 minutes after the water begins to boil. Drain the cod and season with olive oil, pepper and a few drops of lemon juice.

A great alternative dressimg is green sauce *(see recipe). Instead of cod, in many recipes you can use stockfish, which is cod that has been dried instead of salted, and therefore needs longer soaking and longer cooking times.*

FRITTURA MISTA DI PESCE
Mixed fried fish

Saltwater fish for frying, 1 kg - Wheat flour, 200 g
1 lemon - Oil for deep-frying - Salt

One can fry any sort of fresh fish, such as anchovies and sardines, or silversides, mullet, hakes and so on: the condition is that they are of a suitable size for deep-frying, and therefore quite small.

Clean the fish removing the entrails, wash, dry on absorbent paper towel, then dredge with flour and deep-fry a few at a time in plenty of hot oil, until they are golden and crispy. Gradually take them out with the skimmer and place them to drain on absorbent paper towel, sprinkling with salt and a squeeze of lemon.

Fried fish is best when warm, but is good even cold .

PESCE LESSO
Boiled fish

Fish for boiling, 800 g - 1 carrot - 1 onion
1 celery stalk - Parsley - Salt

Fish, like meat, has to be boiled in water flavoured with the canonical stock herbs. Among fish for boiling, we suggest in particular dogfish, but among the many existing types we would also mention hake, gurnard, mullet, scorpionfish, croaker and so on.

Put the herbs in cold water, bring it to the boil, add the cleaned fish and let simmer, with the heat at minimum, for less than a half an hour.

Boiled fish can be dressed with plenty of green sauce *(see recipe). The cooking juices, once filtered, are a good basis for the preparation of other fish-based dishes, for example seafood risotto or rice with freshwater fish.*

SOGLIOLE AL PIATTO
Soles à l'assiette

4 sole, 1 kg - Parsley - 1 garlic clove
1 lemon - Olive oil - Salt and pepper

Put a pot of water on the heat until it is boiling moderately. Arrange the cleaned and lightly salted sole on a plate greased with oil to prevent them from sticking during cooking. Cover the plate with another upturned plate, and place both on the top of the boiling pot: leave the plate in this position for about a quarter of an hour, after which you can dress the sole with chopped garlic and parsley, a drizzle of oil, salt, pepper and lemon juice, and serve.

SOGLIOLE ALLA MUGNAIA
Sole miller style

4 soles, 1 kg - Wheat flour, 200 g - 1 garlic clove - Parsley
Olive oil - Salt and pepper

The sole should be well cleaned and skinned. Flour them and lay in a pan with 3 tablespoons of olive oil, chopped garlic and parsley. Cook for 10 minutes in total over a gentle heat, leaving the sole moist, not dried out and just golden.

Before serving, season with salt and pepper and sprinkle with more chopped fresh parsley.

According to culinary manuals, sole Miller's style, duly skinned should be dipped in milk and flour and then browned in butter and finished with lemon juice and parsley, but according to Granny, millers have different habits, and judging by the result...

SOGLIOLE FRITTE
Fried sole

4 sole, 1 kg - Breadcrumbs, 200 g - 1 lemon
Oil for deep-frying - Salt and pepper

Clean, wash and dry the sole. Coat them in breadcrumbs (not flour!) and deep-fry them, one at a time, in plenty of hot oil.

Remove them golden and crisp with a skimmer, and place to dry on absorbent paper towel, sprinkling with salt. Serve with a drizzle of lemon juice.

TONNO ALLA LIVORNESE
Tuna fish Leghorn style

Tuna fish in oil, 500 g - 3 potatoes
2 garlic cloves
Tomato pulp, 250 g
Parsley - Olive oil
Salt and pepper

Peel the potatoes, slice in rounds and fry them in a pan with a little oil until golden: drain them and salt (a little). Chop garlic and parsley and put them to sweat in another pan: add tomato and the tuna fish, drained and crumbled, and cook for about 10 minutes. Then add the potatoes and cook for another 5 minutes, seasoning with salt and pepper. After cooking, sprinkle the dish with a little chopped fresh parsley.

MEAT

ARISTA ARROSTO
Roast pork loin

Loin of pork with the bone, 1 kg
4 garlic cloves
Rosemary - Florets of wild fennel
Olive oil
Salt and pepper

Slit the loin in correspondence of the ribs, without detaching them completely, but simply separating them from the meat, so that they do not impede cooking and at the same time transmit their flavour.

Baste the loin making small holes in it with a sharp knife, filling the slits with half a clove of garlic, salt, pepper and chopped rosemary: tie it with kitchen twine and roast in a high-sided pan with 4 tablespoons of olive oil and a floret of fennel, for about three quarters of an hour.

You can add some raw potatoes cut into chunks and roasted in the gravy of the pork, as soon as it has finished cooking, or even added during cooking. Usually roast pork loin is cooked in the oven (in this case it is better not to pierce it, but to place the seasoning between the ribs and the meat), cooking it for 2 hours at 160 °C and making sure it does not dry out. However, even in the pan, as Granny cooks it, it is exquisite. Roast pork loin is good either cold or hot, so if you do not consume it immediately after it is roasted, do not heat it when you serve it again at the table.

BISTECCA[6] ALLA FIORENTINA
Florentine beef steak

A T-bone beef steak, 1 kg
Salt

The beef steak must be cut quite high: don't wash it before cooking. Cook on hot embers, but without flame, on both sides for 5 minutes each, and standing on the bone for 5 minutes more. Before and during cooking do not add anything: further, do not pierce it with a fork, so that the internal juices do not escape or evaporate.

The beef steak must remain pink and juicy inside. Add salt only at the end of cooking. It has to be consumed hot, because as it starts cooling it loses much of its flavour.

A perfect match, to my taste, are fried potatoes *(see recipe) and salad, but also a nice plate of beans with olive oil does not clash.*

If you don't have a suitable place to make a fire and don't want to give up on the steak, you can be satisfied even with an electric griddle or a pan, accepting however, that the result cannot be of the same quality as that cooked on embers.

It is clear that this way you have rather to reduce the thickness of your steak. Pork steaks are also excellent grilled, cooked more briefly because naturally thinner, flavoured with some fennel seeds and maybe combined with "Verdure rifatte" *(re-cooked vegetables; see recipe).*

---

[6] The Italian term "bistecca" derives just from the English "beef steak" with just a slight adjustment to the pronunciation.

BOLLITO MISTO
Mixed boiled meat

Mix of beef and poultry (fat and lean beef, hen or capon, etc.), 1 kg
1 carrot - 1 onion - 1 celery stalk - 2 garlic cloves
4 cherry tomatoes - Parsley - Salt

Put the herbs in a pot with about 4 litres of cold water, rightly salted, and place on the heat. When the water is at full boil, add the meat. When it returns to the boil, lower the heat and simmer for an hour, until fully cooked. Boiled meat can be eaten either hot or cold: the perfect dressing is *green sauce* (see recipe).

The difference between cooking boiled meat and making meat stock (see recipe) is that for the latter the meat is set to cook in cold water, so that it can release its substances, flavouring the stock, while in the first case, thanks to the sealing determined by heat, the flavours of the meats will be better preserved inside them. Speaking of poultry, we recommend not depriving the animals of the skin and the heads with wattles and crests, because they are a real treat.

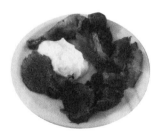

BRACIOLE AGLIO E FINOCCHIO
Garlic and fennel chops

4 tender beef slices (silverside or similar cut), 700 g - 2 garlic cloves
Florets of wild fennel - White wine - Olive oil - Salt and pepper

Heat the oil in a pan with the garlic cloves and a little crumbled floret of fennel: add the slices of meat and a splash of white wine and cook over medium heat, on both sides, for about 20 minutes in all, seasoning with salt and pepper. Serve the chops sprinkled with their cooking sauce.

BRACIOLE ALLA PIZZAIOLA
Beef chops, Pizza style

4 tender beef slices (silverside or similar cut), 700 g
2 salted anchovies - Tomato pulp, 200 g - Drained pickled capers, 20 g
Oregano - Olive oil - Salt

Wash the anchovies, dry and chop finely, add them to the tomato in a pan with 3 tablespoons of olive oil, and allow the flavours to blend slowly. After 5 minutes, add the meat, season with salt and pepper: cook the beef chops on both sides for 10 minutes in total, adding capers and a pinch of oregano when you turn them. Serve sprinkled with their cooking sauce.

Compared to the traditional Pizza style, the addition of anchovies is a brilliant alternative.

BRACIOLE FRITTE
Fried beef chops

4 beef slices (topside or similar cut), 700 g - 3 eggs
Breadcrumbs, 200 g
Oil for deep-frying - Salt

If the chops are too thick, it's better to flatten them with a meat mallet on a wooden chopping board. Dip meat slices in the beaten egg and then dredge with breadcrumbs. Deep-fry them one or two at a time in plenty of hot oil, removing with a skimmer as they turn golden: lay on paper towel to drain, and salt to taste.

Their natural accompaniment is fried potatoes *(see recipe), or a nice fresh green Radicchio (Italian chicory) seasoned with oil and vinegar. Fried beef chops are excellent sprinkled with* anchovy sauce *(see recipe), with the foresight to use plenty of oil to obtain a fairly liquid sauce.*

⮜❧⮞

BRACIOLE RIFATTE
Fried beef chops in tomato sauce

4 fried beef chops
2 garlic cloves
Tomato pulp, 300 g
Parsley - Olive oil

When fried beef chops are left over, it is customary to "re-cook" them with tomato: they are so good that it is suspected that generations of housewives have, where possible, deliberately made sure they were left over to produce this authentic delicacy.

First, prepare the sauce, sautéing chopped garlic and parsley in oil for a few minutes and then adding the tomato pulp. Reduce and amalgamate the flavour over a lively heat: after 5 minutes, add the fried chops and re-cook over low heat for a good quarter of an hour.

Obviously, if you do not have at disposal any leftover fried chops, they can be prepared specially following the previous recipe for fried beef chops.

CERVELLO FRITTO
Deep-fried beef brain

Beef brain, 700 g - 2 eggs - Flour, 150 g - 1 lemon - Olive oil - Salt

The brain needs to be washed in cold running water, scalded for 5 minutes in lightly salted boiling water, drained, left to cool and "peeled", removing the membrane that covers it. After this, chop it into small pieces like a stew. Dredge them with flour and then dip in the beaten egg. Fry them a few at a time in hot oil, removing them with a perforated spoon as soon as they are golden and crisp: place them on kitchen paper and salt them as you go. If you like, you can also sprinkle some lemon juice.

CHIOCCIOLE IN UMIDO
Snail stew

Snails, 1.5 kg - 2 garlic cloves - Tomato pulp, 350 g
Catmint - Olive oil - Salt

First, the largest snails are the most suitable for this recipe, also known in Tuscany as martinacci. To be cooked, snails will have to be previously purged, keeping them in a bucket covered by a piece of wood heavy enough to prevent them coming out for 8-9 days, fed only with bran, then put still alive into boiling water and skimmed at length.

The real preparation begins with putting them in a pan along with tomato, garlic, catmint and salt, covered with water: boil slowly for 2 or even 3 hours, depending on the size of the snails, adding water gradually as needed. When they are ready, eat them by pulling them out of the shell with a toothpick accompanied with their cooking sauce.

My Grandmother told me the sad sight of the snails climbing the inner walls of the pot attempting a desperate escape from the boiling water. If, like the author, you do not feel up to watching such a scene forget this dish or get yourself invited to eat it already prepared!

COLLO RIPIENO
Stuffed chicken neck

Neck of a hen, chicken or capon
Minced lean beef pulp (or leftover cooked meat), 200 g
An egg - Grated Parmesan cheese - Salt and pepper

Empty the neck by removing the bone and removing the little flesh, to be added to the rest of the filling (this delicate operation could be successfully delegated to your butcher). Make a mixture of meat, egg and grated cheese, adding salt and pepper: fill the neck with it and sew up the ends with a needle and strong thread. Boil it slowly for about an hour in *meat stock* or *chicken stock* (see recipe), or in a *vegetable stock* (see recipe) specially prepared. When it is boiled, slice and serve: it also tastes great when cold, with a good mayonnaise.

CONIGLIO ARROSTO
Roast rabbit

A rabbit ready for cooking, 1.2 kg - Rosemary - White wine - Olive oil - Salt

Cut the rabbit into pieces not too small (about a dozen), salt and fry in a pan with olive oil and rosemary. As soon as they are coloured, add half a glass of white wine and continue cooking on medium heat for about an hour, adding water if necessary, i.e. as the meat starts to stick to the pan. Salt to taste.

CONIGLIO ALLA CACCIATORA
Rabbit hunter style

1 rabbit ready for cooking, 1.2 kg
1 carrot - 1 onion - 1 celery stalk
2 garlic cloves - A handful of black olives - Rosemary
Tomato puree (see below)
Red wine - Olive oil - Salt and pepper

Cut the rabbit into pieces not too small (about a dozen). Chop onion, celery, carrot, garlic and rosemary: sauté in a pan with 4 tablespoons of olive oil. After a few minutes, add the rabbit pieces and let them brown: after a few more minutes, add a tablespoon of tomato and pour in half a glass of red wine. Continue cooking on medium heat for about an hour, adding hot water if necessary, i.e. as the meat starts to stick to the pan: season with salt and pepper. Towards the end of cooking, add black olives and salt to taste.

CONIGLIO FRITTO
Fried rabbit

1 rabbit ready for cooking, 1.2 kg - 3 eggs
Flour, 150 g - 1 lemon
Olive oil for frying - Salt

Cut the rabbit into pieces, dredge them with flour and then dip in the beaten egg. Fry a few at a time in hot oil and remove when golden using a perforated spoon, placing them on kitchen paper, salting them as you go. Savour them hot: if you like, a squeeze of lemon is appropriate.

CONIGLIO IN UMIDO
Rabbit stew

1 rabbit ready for cooking, 1.2 kg
Minced lean beef, 300 g
1 carrot - 1 onion - 1 celery stalk
2 garlic cloves - Tomato puree (see below)
Parsley - Red wine - Olive oil - Salt and pepper

Cut the rabbit into pieces not too small (about a dozen). Sauté in 4 tablespoons of olive oil chopped garlic, onion, carrot, celery and parsley. Add the rabbit cut into pieces and the minced beef. Pour in half a glass of red wine, and allow it to reduce a little, then add a tablespoon of tomato and cook slowly for about an hour, adding salt and pepper. If you have some *meat sauce* (see recipe) already prepared you can satisfactorily use it instead of the minced beef.

CONIGLIO ALLA CONTADINA
Rabbit farmer style

1 rabbit ready for cooking, 1.2 kg
Tomato puree, 200 g
1 garlic clove - Rosemary
White wine - Olive oil - Salt and pepper

Cut the rabbit into pieces not too small (about a dozen). Sauté the peeled garlic in a pan with 4 tablespoons of olive oil and a sprig of rosemary; add the rabbit and sauté until it is brown. Pour over half a glass of white wine and allow it to reduce. Finally, add the tomato and cook for about an hour, adding salt and pepper. Add hot water if necessary and turn the rabbit pieces to cook on all sides.

FARAONA ARROSTO
Roast guinea fowl

1 guinea fowl ready for cooking, 1.5 kg - Bacon, 100 g
A handful of black olives - 2 garlic cloves
Rosemary - Sage - Olive oil - Salt and pepper

Chop garlic, sage and rosemary. Make small slits in the skin of the guinea fowl and fill them with the chopped mixture, salt and pepper. Wrap the outside with slices of bacon tied with string. Place it in a large baking pan, well-greased with oil, adding the remaining chopped mixture and a bit of bacon cut into small pieces. Cook for at least an hour: about halfway through the cooking, you can add some peeled potatoes cut into chunks and black olives to cook in the sauce of the guinea fowl.

⌒⌒

FEGATELLI DI MAIALE
Pork livers

Pork liver, 500 g - Pork net (omentum), 200 g - Bay leaves
Breadcrumbs, 150 g - Olive oil - Salt and pepper

The pork net has to be immersed in hot water for a few minutes: drained, dried and cut into squares of about 8-10 cm. Chop the cleaned liver, add some breadcrumbs, salt and pepper and make a smooth mixture. Place small quantities in the middle of the squares of pork net and wrap them well, making roundish small sausages. Roast in a pan with bay leaves for about 20 minutes.

This is a fast and tasty variant on the traditional slow cooking of livers "packaged" in the pork net on skewers, or in the oven, alternated with slices of bread and bay leaves.

FEGATO ALLA FIORENTINA
Florentine liver

Sliced beef liver, 600 g - Flour, 200 g - 2 garlic cloves
Sage - Olive oil - Salt and pepper

Cut the liver in thin slices; season them with salt and pepper and coat them in flour. Heat the oil with the garlic cloves and some sage leaves and when it is hot add the liver, cooking briefly on both sides until it is well coloured on the outside, but not hard.

INVOLTINI DI CARNE
Meat rolls

4 beef slices, 500 g
2 artichokes
Cooked ham, 100 g
4 slices of melting cheese
Tomato puree
Olive oil
Salt and pepper

Remove the tough outer leaves of the artichokes: blanch briefly in boiling water, drain and roughly chop. Beat the slices of beef with a meat mallet on a chopping board. Make the rolls by placing a slice of ham, a slice of melting cheese, a few artichoke leaves, salt and pepper on each slice of meat.

Roll up and secure with a toothpick. Cook the rolls in oil and a tablespoon of tomato for about half an hour, adding water if necessary and turning them to cook on all sides.

LESSO RIFATTO
Reheated boiled beef

Boiled meat for stock (or leftover boiled meat), 600 g
1 carrot - 1 celery stalk - 1 onion - Flour, 100 g
White wine - Olive oil - Salt and pepper

The purpose of this recipe is to reuse the boiled beef used to make meat stock: in fact, it has lost some of its substance and flavour and in this way you can make a dish appetizing again.

Chop carrot, celery and onion and put them in a pan to fry gently in oil. Meanwhile, chop the boiled meat into pieces, flour it and when the vegetables are soft add it to the mixture. Pour over half a glass of white wine, add a little water, season with salt and pepper and let it slowly reduce until the boiled meat is immersed in a tasty sauce.

This formula seems to be more rich and varied than the canonical recipe, where the boiled meat is joined only by a few chopped onions, tomato, garlic and sage, but that is enough to soften it...

MAGRO IN TEGAME
Pot roast beef

Lean beef (rump or shank), 800 g - 4 garlic cloves - Rosemary
Butter - Olive oil - Salt and pepper

Make small holes in the beef with a sharp knife, placing in each half a clove of garlic, salt, pepper and a little butter: massage the piece with salt and pepper. Bind with string as shown in the figure and roast it in a pan, well oiled, for about three quarter of an hour with a sprig of rosemary. When cooked, the meat should be browned on the outside and soft, juicy and pink inside. The beef may be accompanied by some roast potatoes in chunks, added in the pan halfway through cooking. *Florentine peas* (see recipe) are a perfect match.

In Tuscany this recipe is called "rosbiffe", derived precisely from the English roast beef by slightly distorting the pronunciation.

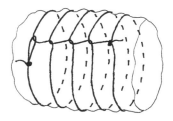

How to tie up the lean beef. Take a piece of string, make a loop at one end and continue from left to right as in the drawing.

PETTI DI POLLO AL PROSCIUTTO COTTO E MOZZARELLA
Chicken breasts with cooked ham and mozzarella (Granny's style)

4 chicken breasts, 500 g - Cooked ham, 100 g
Mozzarella cheese, 100 g - Olive oil - Salt and pepper

Clean the breasts and open them like a book, without separating the two "pages". Fill them with a slice of ham and thin slices of mozzarella, salt and pepper: close them with a toothpick. Sprinkle the outsides too with salt and pepper and cook them in a pan with 4 tablespoons of olive oil for about half an hour, turning halfway through cooking.

PETTI DI POLLO CON LE CIPOLLE
Chicken breasts with onions

4 chicken breasts, 600 g
1 onion - Olive oil - Salt and pepper

Peel the onion and chop not too fine. Put it in a pan with 4 tablespoons of olive oil along with the chicken breasts, add salt and pepper and cook gently for half an hour, add a little warm water if necessary. Naturally, stir the breasts during cooking when necessary.

PICCIONE ARROSTO
Roast pigeon

2 pigeons ready for cooking, 1 kg (in total) - 2 garlic cloves - Sage
Olive oil - Salt and pepper

Rub the pigeons inside with salt and pepper and place a clove of peeled garlic and a sprig of sage in the ventral cavity. Roast for about an hour in a pan with 4 tablespoons of olive oil, so they are well browned on all sides. About halfway through cooking you can add some diced potatoes.

Each of the four diners will get half a pigeon: fate will choose the two lucky ones who will get the heads, which absolutely must not be removed: indeed, they are delicacies for connoisseurs! Using the same procedure you can prepare delicious roasted quail. Since they are much smaller than pigeons, you will need four of them, namely one each.

And now it's time to enjoy a nice chicken, preferably free-range, to which the same recipes described for the rabbit are applied: so we will enjoy it hunter style, roasted in the pan, baked, fried or stewed (see recipes). To cut the chicken into pieces using the special scissors, first you must divide it in two lengthwise, then disconnect the thighs, hips, wings and the breast, in half, without forgetting "the priest's mouthful" (the head). Finally, divide again into two or three parts any pieces that are still quite large.

POLPETTE DI CARNE
Meatballs

Minced lean beef, 300 g - 3 potatoes - 1 egg
Breadcrumbs, 150 g - Parsley
Olive oil - Salt and pepper

Boil the potatoes and peel them hot. Wet your hands and make a mixture of minced beef, boiled potatoes, egg, chopped parsley, salt and pepper: make some round balls, roll them in the breadcrumbs, lightly flatten them and fry them a few at a time in plenty of hot oil. Remove them when crisp and lay to dry on kitchen paper: enjoy hot.

To enrich the flavour of the mixture you can also add a little grated Parmesan cheese. Using the same procedure and the same amounts, replace the minced beef with some finely chopped leftover boiled beef and you can enjoy some delicious boiled beef dumplings.

POLPETTONE
Meatloaf

Minced lean beef, 500 g - Cooked ham, 100 g - 1 egg
Flour, 100 g - Grated Parmesan cheese, 50 g - White wine
Olive oil - Salt and pepper

With wet hands combine the beef with the chopped ham, egg, grated cheese, salt and pepper: form an oblong loaf, dredge it with flour and pan-fry with 5 tablespoons of olive oil for about half an hour, adding half a glass of white wine when nearly cooked. Because the mixture has a tendency to stick easily to the bottom of the pan, turn the meatloaf often enough during cooking. If you need to reduce the cooking time, make two smaller loaves instead of one.

ROSTICCIANA
"Rosticciana" (Pork spare ribs)

Fat and lean pork ribs, 1 kg - Salt and pepper

Very simple: grill the ribs over red-hot embers, but without flames. Salt, pepper and enjoy hot. A natural accompaniment is *grilled sausages* and *reheated vegetables* (see recipes).

SALSICCE AI FERRI
Grilled sausages

8 sausages, 600 g - Salt and pepper (optional)

Put the sausages on the grill and pierce with a fork to drain the fat, making sure that they are well cooked inside (not boiled) and crispy outside. Usually salt and pepper are not needed, but this depends on individual tastes and the composition of the sausages. Highly recommended accompaniments are *reheated vegetables* and *fried potatoes* (see recipes).

SALSICCE E FAGIOLI
Sausages and beans

8 sausages, 600 g - Boiled white beans, 500 g
4 garlic cloves - Tomato puree, 200 g
Sage - Olive oil - Salt and pepper

Pierce the sausages with a fork and brown with garlic and sage in a pan with a little olive oil: add the tomato and the already cooked beans (see the recipe for *beans in oil*) and cook for about 10 minutes. Check salt and pepper, add if necessary.

SPEZZATINO DI MANZO
Beef stew

Beef muscle, 700 g - 1 onion - 2 garlic cloves
Potatoes, 800 g - Tomato puree, 250 g
Fennel seeds - Olive oil - Salt and pepper

Put the garlic cloves and the sliced onion in a pan to sweat with 4 tablespoons of olive oil, then add the muscle cut into small pieces and sauté over a high heat until it is well coloured. Add the tomato, a few fennel seeds, cover with water and let it simmer for about an hour with the lid on, adding salt and pepper. Finally, add the potatoes peeled and cut into chunks letting it reduce for about half an hour, until they are completely boiled.

71

You can also use other cuts of beef, but with muscle this dish is at its best. If you like offal, you can prepare a very unusual lung stew following the same recipe, and simply replacing the muscle with lung.

SPIEDINI ALLA FIORENTINA
Florentine skewers

Mixed meat (pork and pork liver, chicken, rabbit), 600 g
2 sausages - 4 small birds ready for cooking
1 bread stick - Bacon - Bay leaves - Sage
Olive oil - Salt and pepper

Slice the bread and moisten slightly to prevent drying out during cooking. Take the skewers (preferably wooden) and thread on in order: a sage leaf, a slice of bread, a bay leaf, a piece of bacon, a piece chosen from the various meats and so on, until the skewer is full. Season with salt and pepper. Place the skewers on the embers, turning from time to time and brushing with oil, for about half an hour. If you do not have access to a fire, you can put the skewers in a roasting pan and put it in the oven at 180° C for three quarters of an hour.

For hunters it will be easier to procure the small birds (traditionally wrens) and to prepare them, otherwise you will have to order them in good time from your local butcher.

TRIPPA ALLA FIORENTINA
Florentine tripe

Tripe (reticulum and rumen), 800 g
Tomato puree, 250 g - 1 carrot - 1 onion - 1 stalk celery
2 garlic cloves - Parsley
Grated Parmesan cheese - Olive oil
Sal and pepper

For best results, take care to choose either the reticulum or the rumen of the tripe. Cut into fairly thin strips depending on taste, although we suggest making them as thin as possible. Chop garlic, onion, celery, carrot and parsley and sauté in a pan with 4 tablespoons of olive oil. Add the tripe and the tomato, season with salt and pepper and cook slowly for a good half hour, stirring continuously. If necessary, reduce a little more so that the tripe is not too soupy. Tripe is eaten strictly hot. Serve with a good sprinkling of grated cheese.

The beauty of this dish, as known, is that, despite being made with cuts of beef considered waste, it reveals a superb taste. The tomato puree can be replaced with 400 g of Florentine ribbed tomatoes, lengthening the cooking time by about 10 minutes: the result is even better.

ZAMPONE E FAGIOLI
Trotter and beans

1 pork trotter, 800 g
White beans already boiled, 500 g
Olive oil - Salt and pepper

Pierce the trotter here and there with a pointed skewer, to allow some of the fat to escape during cooking, wrap it in a cloth and tie with string at both ends. Boil the bundle for about 3 hours starting with cold water and serve cut into not too thin slices along with boiled beans seasoned with olive oil, salt and pepper.

Trotter, like cotechino, should be strictly eaten hot. If you use cotechino, cooking time is reduced to about one hour. Beans can be replaced with lentils, which have to be boiled for about one hour in salt water without being steeped and can be seasoned in the same way as the beans.

EGGS

The omelette is a very versatile preparation that can be made with a huge range of ingredients in addition to eggs: in short, if you do not know what to do with something, then you can make an omelette with it! Therefore, the omelettes described below are only a tiny selection of all those known in Tuscany and beyond.

To cook an omelette you can follow two philosophies: there are those who turn it and those who do not. In any case, as soon as the egg is set it is a good idea to pierce the omelette with a fork and lift it a bit, so that the still liquid egg falls to the bottom of the pan. It will then be the cook to decide whether to turn or not, although we suggest not and, for this reason, you should choose a pan large enough to make a thin omelette.

You know what? I think I shall make an omelette...

FRITTATA COI VITALBINI
Clematis shoot omelette

8 eggs - Vitalbini (shoots of Clematis), 200 g
Olive oil - Salt and pepper

You can only make this omelette if you can procure the spring shoots of a climbing shrub that grows spontaneously throughout Italy, called Clematis vitalba. But we ought to warn you that Clematis is a toxic plant that can cause skin irritation on contact, so that you must be careful when collecting the shoots and only con-

sume small quantities. Not surprisingly, tradition suggests using only the shoots, because the toxins accumulate only in the older parts of the plant.

Peel the vitalbini and blanch briefly in boiling water, drain and dry. Break the eggs into a large bowl, beat them thoroughly: add the vitalbini and season with salt and pepper. Put a well-oiled pan on the heat, cook the omelette and enjoy it hot.

FRITTATA DELLA MI'NONNA
Grandma's omelette

6 eggs - Bread crumb, 100 g - Milk, 2 dl - Olive oil - Salt and pepper

Naturally an omelette can be made even without adding anything to the eggs, but if you want to give it more texture you can copy my Grandmother. Put a little bread crumb to soak in the milk and then add it crumbled to the beaten eggs, measuring salt and pepper. Proceed as in the previous recipe and enjoy.

FRITTATA DI ASPARAGI
Asparagus omelette

6 eggs - 8 asparagus - Olive oil - Salt and pepper

Trim the hardest part of the stem off from asparagus; tie them in a bunch and boil them standing in hot boiling water for 10 minutes. As soon as they are ready, cut into pieces about one cm long and put them in a frying pan greased with oil, then pour over the beaten eggs with salt and pepper and cook the omelette.

FRITTATA DI CARCIOFI
Artichoke omelette

6 eggs - 4 violet artichokes
Flour, 80 g
Olive oil - Salt and pepper

Remove the larger outer leaves from the artichokes, cut off the tips, then cut them in half and slice into strips, flour and fry lightly in a pan with 3 tablespoons of olive oil for a quarter of an hour. Beat the eggs and pour over the artichokes: season with salt and pepper and cook the omelette.

FRITTATA DI CIPOLLE (O PORRI)
Onion (or leek) omelette

6 eggs - 2 onions (or 2 leeks) - Olive oil
Salt and pepper

Cut the onions (or leeks) into thin slices and brown them in a pan with 3 tablespoons of olive oil for a quarter of an hour. Beat the eggs and pour over the onions: season with salt and pepper and cook the omelette.

FRITTATA DI PATATE
Potato omelette

6 eggs - 2 potatoes
Olive oil - Salt and pepper

Peel the potatoes, cut into thin slices or very small chunks. Cook them until golden in a pan for about 20 minutes and then add the beaten eggs. Add salt and pepper and your omelette is ready.

FRITTATA DI VERDURE
Vegetable omelette

6 eggs - Chard, spinach or leaf vegetables, 500 g - Olive oil
Salt and pepper

Peel the vegetables and boil in salted water for about 10 minutes: finely chop them and sauté in a pan with a little oil for a few minutes. Beat the eggs, pour them over the vegetables adding salt and pepper and move the mixture gently with a wooden fork until it has set.

We suggest not mixing different types of vegetables for the same omelette, but choosing only one type to better savour the flavour.

FRITTATA DI ZUCCHINE
Courgette (zucchini) omelette

6 eggs - 2 small courgettes
Olive oil - Salt and pepper

Wash the courgettes, cut into slices and put them to fry in a pan with a film of oil. When they start to sweat, add the beaten eggs, salt and pepper and move the mixture gently with a fork until it has set.

Following a similar procedure you can also use just the courgette flowers instead of the courgettes themselves.

UOVA AFFRITTELLATE
Scrambled eggs

8 eggs - Olive oil - Salt and pepper

Put the oil to heat in a pan and when it is hot, break the eggs directly into it. Add salt, pepper and stir the eggs vigorously while they are setting.

UOVA AL POMODORO
Tomato eggs

6 eggs - Tomato puree (or sauce), 200 g - Basil
Olive oil - Salt and pepper

Put the tomatoes to warm in oil with a few basil leaves. When hot break the eggs directly set into it: the ideal is to allow the whites to set, stirring them, and leave the yolks intact. However, if you like, you can break and stir the yolks too. Add salt and pepper and serve with plenty of good bread for dipping.

Alternatively, following the traditional recipe, which is a bit longer but equally excellent, you can sauté some juicy Florentine ribbed tomatoes in oil and garlic and then, after about 10 minutes, add the eggs, concluding with a sprig of basil.

<hr />

UOVA AL TEGAMINO
Fried eggs

8 eggs - Olive oil - Salt and pepper

The preparation is apparently so obvious that it could seem not worth writing, but some people say that talent in the kitchen can be recognized precisely by how someone can fry an egg, so do not underestimate this recipe!

For an excellent result you need to cook the eggs no more than two at a time in a well-oiled pan: when the oil is hot, you break the eggs, letting the whites drop but keeping the yolks in the shell. Once the white is set, then the yolk can be placed in the centre, not letting it cook but simply gloss over, adding a pinch of salt and pepper.

UOVA SODE CON L'ACCIUGATA
Hard-boiled eggs with anchovy sauce

8 eggs
Anchovy sauce (see recipe)

Boil the eggs by putting them in a saucepan with cold water and boiling for 8-10 minutes from when you turn on the heat (if you put straight into boiling water they may break).

If you boil them for 8 minutes the yolk will remain semi-liquid in the centre, while after 10 minutes it will be completely solid. Peel the eggs when they are still warm, cut into slices and sprinkle with the *anchovy sauce.*

The combination of the flavour of anchovy and boiled egg makes this dish a delicacy for connoisseurs. Anchovy sauce can be effectively replaced with green sauce *(see recipe) made with the addition of chopped capers.*

VEGETABLE DISHES AND GARNISHES

BUGLIONE DI ZUCCHINE
Courgette (zucchini) soup

12 courgettes - Half an onion - Artichokes (optional)
Tomato puree, 100 g - Olive oil - Salt and pepper

Slice the courgettes and put them to fry in a pan with 4 tablespoons of olive oil along with the onion not too finely chopped (leeks are equally good) and, if desired, also an artichoke deprived of the hardest leaves. Add a few tablespoons of tomato, season with salt and pepper, and leave to cook slowly for about half an hour.

CARCIOFI FRITTI
Fried artichokes

4 artichokes - 2 eggs - Flour, 150 g
Olive oil - Salt

Artichokes, whatever the recipe, must be steeped for a few minutes in water made acidic with lemon juice to avoid oxidation, drained and dried properly so they do not retain too much moisture among the bracts.

Remove the stalks and the tough outer leaves of the artichokes, trim the tips and cut them vertically into four quarters. Dredge with flour, then dip in beaten egg and fry a few at a time in plenty of hot oil, removing them gradually using a perforated spoon: set to dry on absorbent kitchen paper salting as you go. They are best enjoyed hot, but they are good even cold.

CARCIOFI RIFATTI
Reheated artichokes

4 artichokes - 1 garlic clove
Parsley - Olive oil - Salt and pepper

Acidulate the artichokes (see previous recipe) then cut off the stalks leaving a small part cleaned of hair, trim the tips and then cut vertically into four quarters. Chop garlic and parsley and put everything to cook in a pan with olive oil for about a quarter of an hour.

CARCIOFI RIPIENI
Stuffed artichokes

4 artichokes - Tuna fish in water, 150 g - 1 garlic clove - Parsley
Breadcrumbs - Olive oil - Salt and pepper

Acidulate the artichokes (see previous recipe) then cut off the stalks, trim the tips and remove the innermost leaves, leaving a cavity to be filled with the filling. For the latter proceed as for *stuffed tomatoes* (see recipe).

CAVOLFIORE LESSO
Boiled cauliflower

1 cauliflower - 1 lemon - Olive oil - Salt and pepper

Boil the whole cauliflower for about half an hour, in salted water, until it is soft enough to pierce with a fork. Divide into florets and season with olive oil, lemon, pepper and adjust salt to taste. It is good either hot or cold.

CAVOLFIORE STRASCICATO
Dragged[7] cauliflower

1 cauliflower - 1 sausage - 2 garlic cloves
A floret (or seeds) of wild fennel - Tomato puree
Olive oil - Salt and pepper

Divide the cauliflower into florets: put them in a pan with olive oil, garlic, fennel and a tablespoon of tomato. If there are some leaves attached to the cauliflower do not throw away, but add them too because they enrich the dish. Skin the sausage, break it up with a fork and add to the cauliflower.

---

[7] The meaning of "dragged" is the same as for *Pasta dragged in meat sauce* (see recipe).

To get a more intense flavour you can sauté the ingredients in the cooking juices of a pork steak or roast pork loin *(see recipe), since the flavour matches perfectly with cauliflower, as well if not better than sausages.*

FAGIOLI ALL'OLIO
Beans in oil

Cannellini beans, 500 g (200 g if dried)
1 garlic clove - Sage
Olive oil
Salt and pepper

If the beans are dried they have to be previously soaked for half a day and in weight should be little less than a half of what is required if they are fresh. Put the beans in a pot of cold salted water with garlic and some sage leaves boil slowly with the lid on for about 2 hours. Take care that the boil occurs at a very low heat, so that the skin of the beans breaks to the minimum. Once cooked, drain the beans and season with plenty of oil, salt and pepper.

They are delicious either hot or cold, but hot they give of their best. Just as good are chickpeas in oil, *prepared in the same way.*

86

FAGIOLI ALL'UCCELLETTO
Beans in tomato sauce

Boiled white beans, 500 g
3 garlic cloves - Tomato puree, 100 g
Sage - Olive oil - Salt and pepper

To boil the beans follow the previous recipe. Put the garlic in the oil to turn golden, then add the beans, tomato puree and sage and cook slowly for about a quarter of an hour.

FAGIOLI, TONNO E CIPOLLA
Beans, tuna fish and onion

Boiled white beans, 400 g - Tuna fish in water, 300 g
4 spring onions - Olive oil
Salt and pepper

Although this is a combination rather than a preparation, in terms of goodness and popularity among Tuscan people it deserves the rank of recipe. And what a recipe!

Boil the beans according the recipe for *beans in oil*: mix them with the drained and chopped tuna fish, add the chopped onions and season with good oil, salt and pepper.

The onion can also be red, but spring onions are really ideal. It is better to use tuna fish in water rather than in oil because of the poor quality of the oils generally used which as well as adding to the calories of the dish may ruin the taste.

FAGIOLINI VERDI AL POMODORO
Runner beans in tomato sauce

Runner beans, 400 g - Tomato puree, 200 g - 1 garlic clove
Olive oil - Salt

Sauté the garlic in a pan with 3 tablespoons of olive oil, and then add the tomato and the beans which have been previously trimmed and washed. The cooking takes about half an hour: add the salt.

FAGIOLINI VERDI LESSI
Boiled runner beans

Runner beans, 400 g - 1 garlic clove - 1 lemon - Olive oil - Salt

Trim the beans top and bottom and wash them. Boil by immersing in boiling salted water but not for too long, just until they are soft enough to pierce with a fork. At the end they should still be nicely green and rich in flavour. Season with olive oil, finely-chopped raw garlic and lemon juice.

FINOCCHI IN BIANCO
Fennel

2 large fennel bulbs
2 garlic cloves
Sage - Olive oil - Salt and pepper

For this dish, large fennel bulbs are better than the smaller ones. Put the garlic cloves and the sage to sweat in oil in a pan. Wash the fennel, remove the stalks and green leaves and slice vertically along the veins. Add a little water and leave to cook for about half an hour.

MELANZANE AL PARMIGIANO
Parmesan cheese aubergines

4 medium aubergines - 2 garlic cloves
Tomato puree, 250 g
Basil - Grated Parmesan cheese - Olive oil
Fine and coarse salt, pepper

Cut the aubergines into slices: put them on a plate and sprinkle with coarse salt. Put another plate on top with a weight on it, and leave for about 2 hours to remove the water. Remove the salt by washing, dry well and fry lightly in a pan with some oil, then place on kitchen paper to dry. Cook them in another pan for about half an hour with garlic, chopped basil, tomato and olive oil, add salt and pepper. Once cooked sprinkle with grated cheese.

The name is a jocular reference to the famous eggplant Parmigiana that is eaten in Naples, made in the oven with lots of tomato sauce and lashings of cheese.

MELANZANE FRITTE DORATE
Fried aubergines

4 medium aubergines
Flour, 200 g
Olive oil for frying
Fine and coarse salt

Prepare the aubergines as described in the previous recipe to take away their acidity. Wash off the salt, dredge with flour and fry a few at a time in plenty of hot oil until they are golden: put them on kitchen paper to dry off excess oil. We recommend not peeling the aubergines.

PATATE ALLA CONTADINA
Potatoes farmer style

Potatoes, 800 g
Tomato preserve (see recipe)
Fennel seeds
Olive oil
Salt and pepper

Peel the potatoes, cut into chunks and place in a pan with a tablespoon of tomato preserve, a pinch of fennel seeds, olive oil, salt and pepper. Cover all with water and put the pot over the fire until you can pierce the potatoes with a fork. You may need to add more water during the cooking.

If you do not like fennel you can replace it with rosemary. The traditional recipe for this potato dish uses sage, but the idea of flavouring with fennel seeds is brilliant.

PATATE FRITTE
Fried potatoes

Yellow potatoes, 700 g - Sage
Olive oil for frying - Salt

Peel the potatoes, cut them into slices no more than half a cm thick and fry a few at a time in plenty of hot oil. Along with fried potatoes you can also fry beautiful sage leaves that will turn crisp and crumbly. Salt them after frying, place on kitchen paper and eat hot. They are an ideal accompaniment to *Florentine beef steak* (see recipe).

PATATE LESSE
Boiled potatoes

Potatoes, 800 g - 2 garlic cloves - Parsley - Olive oil - Salt

Boil the potatoes, peel while still warm and cut into chunks. Chop garlic and parsley and use to season the potatoes along with necessary amount of oil and salt.

Also excellent are potatoes baked under ashes (for those who have a fireplace) as recalled by my mother who came from the hills of the Tuscan-Romagnolo Apennines: the potatoes are covered with ashes mixed with burning embers. When cooked they can be peeled and garnished in one of many possible ways.

PEPERONATA
Peppers

4 red and yellow peppers - 1 onion - Tomato puree, 250 g
Olive oil - Salt

Cut the peppers into strips, not too big and put them to cook with olive oil, tomato and onion chopped into slices and salt. Cooking takes about half an hour and is completed when the peppers are completely soft.

PISELLI ALLA FIORENTINA
Florentine peas

Peas, 600 g - Bacon, 100 g
4 garlic cloves - Sugar
Olive oil - Salt

Put the garlic and the bacon to brown in oil in a saucepan. After a few minutes, add the raw peas, a teaspoon of sugar and a little hot water or vegetable stock. After a quarter of an hour the peas are ready and can be salted just before the end of cooking.

POLENTA FRITTA
Fried cornmeal

Cornmeal, 500 g (see recipe)
Olive oil for frying
Salt

For the preparation of *cornmeal* follow the recipe. Cut it into slices not too high and then into small rectangles, and fry in the necessary amount of hot oil. Let them dry on kitchen paper, salt to taste and enjoy.

POLPETTE DI PATATE
Potato balls

Boiled potatoes, 500 g - 1 egg yolk - 1 garlic clove
Grated Parmesan cheese, 60 g - Breadcrumbs, 150 g
Parsley - Basil - Olive oil for frying - Salt

Chop garlic, basil and parsley. Mix the peeled potatoes, the egg yolk, the grated cheese and the chopped herbs and garlic, season with salt and form the mixture into small, round slightly flat balls. Coat in breadcrumbs and fry until nicely golden. Let them dry on kitchen paper, add salt and enjoy.

POMODORI GRATINATI
Grilled tomatoes

4 ripe salad tomatoes - 1 garlic clove - Parsley
Breadcrumbs, 100 g - Olive oil - Salt and pepper

Cut the tomatoes in two horizontally and remove the seeds. Dribble the tomatoes with oil and sprinkle with breadcrumbs and chopped garlic and parsley. Place them on the grill, adjusting salt and pepper to taste. As soon as they are soft they are ready.

POMODORI RIPIENI
Stuffed tomatoes

4 ripe salad tomatoes - Tuna fish in water, 150 g - 1 garlic clove
Parsley - Breadcrumbs, 50 g - Olive oil - Salt and pepper

Cut the tomatoes in half horizontally and remove the seeds. Prepare the filling with chopped drained tuna fish, garlic, parsley, salt and pepper, to which you can add breadcrumbs to give it more volume and texture. Fill the half tomatoes and put them to cook in a pan with a little oil over low heat until the skin is soft. Stuffed onions can be made in the same way.

PORCINI ALLA BRACE
Grilled porcino mushrooms

Porcino mushrooms (caps only), 500 g - 2 garlic cloves
Olive oil - Salt and pepper

For this dish, we use only the caps of the mushrooms, so when you buy them you should choose those with large caps. The stems can be reused for other dishes, such as sautéed mushrooms.

Wild mushrooms from the woods (unlike champignon) should be cleaned only by dusting and moistening, without washing them. Take the caps, make some slits on the top and put in small slices of garlic, season with salt and roast them on the grill top and bottom. If you like, add a little olive oil after cooking.

PORCINI FRITTI
Fried porcino mushrooms

Porcino mushrooms (caps only), 500 g - 2 eggs
Flour, 150 g - Olive oil for frying - Salt

For this recipe too it is better to use large porcino mushrooms. Slice both the caps and the stalks, and dip first in the flour and then in the beaten egg. Fry a few at a time in the necessary amount of hot oil. It is important that the frying should be

95

lively but very short. Drain, dry on kitchen paper and season with salt. They are best savoured when eaten hot.

PORCINI TRIFOLATI
Sauteed mushrooms

Porcino mushrooms, 500 g - 2 garlic cloves - Catmint - Olive oil - Salt

For this recipe is not necessary to use large and well-formed mushrooms. Chop both the caps and the stalk into not too small pieces and put them to cook in a pan with garlic, catmint leaves and oil for about 10 minutes. Of course, you can also prepare other varieties of mushrooms in this way.

Porcino mushrooms prepared according to this recipe can also be used as a sauce for pasta: take care to chop them very fine, possibly leaving some strips for embellishment.

PURÈ DI PATATE
Potato puree

Potatoes, 500 g - Butter, 40 g - Milk, 2 dl - Salt

Boil the potatoes, peel them and pass them through a food mill. Put them in a saucepan with the butter and the milk. Stir continuously until you get a creamy mixture: in the meantime add salt.

VALIGETTE DI VERZA
Savoy cabbage cases

Half a savoy cabbage - 2 courgettes - Leftover boiled meat, 150 g
Cooked ham, 50 g - Tomato puree, 150 g
4 slices of melting cheese - Olive oil - Salt

Cut the courgettes into thin slices and brown in oil. Add tomato, leftover boiled meat and the courgettes mashing everything with a little oil and salt until you have a sort of paste. Prepare the "cases" with large cabbage leaves that you have previously blanched slightly, on which you lay a layer of the paste, a slice of ham and a little melting cheese. Roll them up and fasten with toothpicks. Finally, finish cooking the "cases" in a pan with 3 tablespoons of olive oil.

The secret and the usefulness of the "cases" is that the filling can also be made with other ingredients, such as cold cuts, various meats and leftover vegetables.

HOW TO BOIL VEGETABLES

Trim and wash the vegetables as needed: cook them in boiling salted water until "al dente", taking care not to overcook, so that they retain all their flavour. Obviously, the time will be different depending on the type of vegetable. Furthermore, the cooking water should be the minimum required, in order not to unnecessarily absorb the substance from vegetables. If the water is reduced during boiling, add boiling water from a separate saucepan. Season the boiled vegetables with the necessary amount of olive oil and salt.

A trick to boil courgettes is to cut them into small pieces before: in this way the boiling time will be shorter than that for whole courgettes and so the taste will be better preserved. Tasting is believing.

꧂

'VERDURE RIFATTE
Reheated vegetables

Boiled vegetables
(spinach, chard, chicory, wild herbs, turnips, etc.), 500 g
2 garlic cloves - Olive oil - Salt

Boil the vegetables following the previous recipe: sautè briefly over a high heat in oil with a little garlic already golden. Add salt.

They are an excellent side dish for grilled sausages and pork steak. In order to enjoy the aroma of each variety of vegetable at its best, we suggest to "reheat" one at a time.

ZUCCHINE RIPIENE
Stuffed courgettes

8 round zucchini - Leftover boiled meat, 300 g - 1 onion
1 garlic clove - Tomato puree - Basil
Parsley - Breadcrumbs, 80 g
Olive oil - Salt

Open the zucchini by cutting a slice horizontally near the top, and scoop out the inside with a teaspoon. Prepare the filling by chopping leftover boiled meat, part of the zucchini pulp, basil, parsley, garlic, salt and pepper. Fill the zucchini finishing the filling with a layer of breadcrumbs and then close with the "hat". Begin cooking in oil with some chopped onion, add the tomato and water gradually to prevent sticking: salt to taste.

The boiled meat can be replaced by browned ground beef or tuna fish.

CAKES, SWEETMEATS, ETC.

BALLOTTE
Boiled chestnuts

Chestnuts, 1 kg - A floret of fennel - Salt

Shell the chestnuts and boil them for about one hour and a half with a sprig of fennel and a little salt. When they are sufficiently cooled, but still warm, remove the inner membrane too and enjoy. They are good either hot or cold.

BRUCIATE
Roast chestnuts

Chestnuts, 1 kg

Make a small cut on the skin of the chestnuts to prevent bursting during roasting and to facilitate the shelling. Then place them on the special perforated pan on the grill. If you don't have access to an open fire or a barbecue, a gas or electric hob will do.

After about 20 minutes, when the skin is well browned, remove from heat and peel. Best served hot. Grappa is a perfect accompaniment.

～⁂～

BRUTTI E BONI

Ground almonds, 500 g
Sugar, 500 g - 4 egg whites
A piece of lemon zest - Vanilla sugar - Rice paper

"Ugly and good" simply means that they don't look good but taste fantastic! Whip the egg whites and add the ground almonds, the lemon zest and the sugar until you have a firm mixture. Take small portions of it with a tablespoon and make some small mounds on the rice paper. Let them rest for a short time and then bake at 160 °C for at least half an hour, until they are darkened. Finally, sprinkle with icing sugar. It is almost a must to have some Vin Santo to accompany the tasting.

～⁂～

CASTAGNACCIO
Chestnut cake

Sweet chestnut flour, 400 g - Pine nuts, 50 g
Walnuts, 50 g - Rosemary
Olive oil - Salt

This cake is also known by the name "migliaccio" and it is traditionally prepared in autumn when the chestnut flour is fresh from the mill. Mix the flour with water and a pinch of salt: the mixture should be quite firm. Scatter the mixture with pine nuts, crushed walnuts and a pinch of rosemary needles. Roll out the mixture in a well oiled low rectangular pan, to a height of about one cm. Bake in the preheated oven at 200 °C for half an hour.

～✑～

CENCI
Rags

Flour, 300 g - 2 eggs
2 spoonfuls of sugar - Butter, 50 g
Icing sugar - Olive oil for frying - Salt

The rags are traditionally prepared during Carnival. Mix the flour, the eggs, the sugar and the butter (not cold and semi melted) with a pinch of salt into a well-mixed dough. Let it stand for an hour and then roll out fairly thin and cut into slightly irregular pieces. Curl them slightly like butterflies and fry in plenty of hot oil, until they are crispy on the outside but soft on the inside.

Place them on kitchen paper and sprinkle with icing sugar (if you don't have it, ordinary sugar will do).

FICATTOLE
Fried dough

Flour, 300 g - Brewer's yeast, 20 g
Sugar (or salt) - Olive oil for frying

Dissolve the yeast in water and pour it into the flour; add a tablespoon of oil and knead into a ball. Cover the dough with a cloth and let it rise for 2 hours. If you do not want to prepare the dough yourself, you can buy it already prepared. Roll out the dough not too thin, cut it into small lozenges and fry in hot oil. Arrange the pastries on kitchen paper and at this point you can choose to sprinkle with plenty of sugar or a little salt. If you choose salt, ficattole can be a great accompaniment to many savoury dishes.

※

FRITTELLE DI MELE
Apple fritters

4 apples - Flour, 100 g
Sugar, 100 g
1 egg
Olive oil for frying

Prepare a not too liquid batter with flour, water and finally the egg. Remove the core of the apples with a corer and cut them horizontally into slices about half a cm high. Dip in the batter and fry in hot oil. Place the fritters on kitchen paper and sprinkle with plenty of sugar.

Typically, these fritters are made with renette apples, but you can also try them with other varieties.

104

FRITTELLE DI RISO
Rice fritters

Pudding rice, 400 g
4 egg yolks and 2 whites - Sugar, 400 g - 1 orange
Milk, 1 l - Flour, as required
Olive oil for frying - Salt

Rice fritters are traditionally prepared for the feast of St. Giovanni which falls on March 19. Boil the rice in the milk and add half the sugar when it boils. Mix the rice with the eggs, the juice of the orange and a pinch of salt. If the consistency of the dough is not stiff enough you can add some flour. Fry the mixture in small portions, using a wet tablespoon, in plenty of hot oil. Once fried, place the fritters on kitchen paper and sprinkle with plenty of sugar.

MARMELLATA DI MORE
Blackberry jam

Blackberries, 1 kg
Sugar, 500 g

Blackberry picking in the summer can be an opportunity for some good outings: collect only those that are, soft and ripe and not those that are still partially green. Wash the blackberries, boil without water until they are almost macerated and add the sugar. Continue boiling until you have a pulp, and then pass it through a food mill. Put the jam into jars while it is still hot, so that as it cools it creates a "vacuum" and hermetically seals the jars. After you have opened a jar you will have to store it in the refrigerator.

MELE COTTE
Baked apples

4 apples (renette or Granny Smith)
Sugar

Put the apples to boil in half a cm water in a pot with a lid that is sealed, so that the heat and the steam does not escape, and is distributed around the apples, cooking them from all sides. Add some sugar to the apples when the skin begins to crack. The cooking time depends on the type of apple, but on average is about 20 minutes. You can cook pears in the same way.

LIQUORE DI MORE
Blackberry liquor

Ripe blackberries, 1 kg - Sugar, 500 g - Alcohol at 90°, 2 l

Wash the blackberries, boil without water until they are almost macerated and add the sugar. Continue boiling until you have a pulp. Spread a clean linen cloth in a container of adequate size, pour in the pulp and draw the corners of the cloth together like a candy. Squeeze the "candy" and collect the filtered liquid in the container. Finally, add the alcohol, stir and hermetically seal the liquor in one or more bottles.

PAN DI RAMERINO
Rosemary bread

Flour, 350 g - Sugar, 50 g - Brewer's yeast, 20 g
Sultanas, 100 g - 1 egg white - Olive oil - Salt

Rosemary bread is traditionally prepared on Holy Thursday of Easter-time. Mix the flour with water, the yeast dissolved in water in a bowl, sugar and a pinch of salt. Knead the dough, cover with a cloth and let it rise for an hour. Knead the dough again, adding three tablespoons of olive oil, the sultanas and a generous pinch of rosemary needles. Make four round loaves, cut a cross on the top of each and let them rise a little longer. Finally, brush them with the egg white to give them shine and bake at 200 °C for half an hour.

HOMEMADE SWEETMEATS

Among the traditional homemade sweetmeats we should remember the snacks made with our good unsalted bread, sometimes more delicious than the most elaborate cakes: bread, butter and sugar *and* bread, wine and sugar *(with strictly red wine). How delicious! If you like, the sugar that accompanies the butter can be replaced by a light sprinkling of salt.*

Bread, butter and sugar   *Bread, wine and sugar*

SCHIACCIATA ALLA FIORENTINA
Florentine flat cake

In this case, we do not give the quantities in grams, but just as they were transmitted to the author.

12 spoonfuls of flour - 10 of milk - 8 of sugar
4 of olive oil - 2 eggs - 1 orange - Brewer's yeast, 20 g
Icing sugar - Butter, 20 g - Salt

Florentine flat cake is traditionally prepared during Carnival. Grate the zest of the orange. Make a mixture in a bowl with the flour, the sugar, the milk, the oil, the eggs, the grated zest, the orange juice, the yeast and a pinch of salt and let it rest for about an hour. Pour the mixture into a rectangular pan greased with the butter: to prevent the flat cake from sticking to the pan you can use the trick of dusting the bottom of the pan with bread crumbs. Bake at 200 °C for half an hour. When cooked, sprinkle the flat cake with the necessary amount of sugar.

Traditionally, a stencil in the shape of the Florentine lily is placed over the cake before dusting with icing sugar to create the design.

SCHIACCIATA CON L'UVA
Bread cake with grapes

Wine grapes, 600 g - Flour, 250 g
Sugar, 100 g - Brewer's yeast, 15 g
Rosemary - Olive oil - Salt

This bread cake is prepared in the autumn at the time of the grape harvest. If you do not want to prepare the bread dough yourself, you can buy 800 g already prepared. Otherwise, mix the flour with water and the yeast, previously dissolved in water, in a bowl. Knead, and cover the dough with a cloth and let it rise for one hour. Knead the dough again, adding half the sugar, a tablespoon of olive oil and a pinch of salt.

Grease a rectangular pan and roll out half of the dough, making sure that it extends beyond the edges by about one cm. Remove the grapes from the bunches, wash them, let them dry and spread half over the dough crushing them a little. Sprinkle with the sugar and trinkle over a little olive oil. With the rest of the dough make a second layer and place it over the first one, and repeat the same steps made with the first with grapes, sugar and oil, then add a pinch of rosemary leaves. Let it rise for another hour and bake at 200 °C for half an hour.

Starting is hard, but then the path will run.
It's your turn now since my own tale is done.

INDEX

First Courses

Fish and Mollusks

Meat

Eggs

Vegetable dishes and garnishes

Cakes, sweetmeats, etc.

Toscani super DOC

"Libri pregevoli e rari, che nessuna Mondadori pubblicherà mai, occupate come sono le grandi case editrici a stampare le idiozie da milioni di copie."

"Books valuable and rare, that no Mondadori will ever print, occupied as the big publishers are in making the most idiot best sellers."

Alessandro Bencistà

A nice roundup of vernacular traditions, music, recipes and anything else survives of the popular culture of Tuscany.

First printed in Florence
at the printworks-publishing house Polistampa
September 2013